With advice
from the
**National
Asthma
Campaign**

Eleanor Archer

FRANKLIN WATTS
NEW YORK•LONDON•SYDNEY

Ada is an athlete. She runs in 100-metre and 200-metre races.

Ada has asthma. This means she sometimes finds it hard to breathe. Ada controls her asthma so it doesn't stop her running.

Ada has two inhalers to control her asthma. She uses the brown one every morning. It's called a 'preventer'. She uses the blue 'reliever' when she has difficulty breathing.

3

To be a top athlete Ada needs to be very fit.
She trains every day, except Sunday.
Today she is training at the track with her coach,
Devon. "Hello!" Ada says.

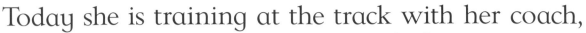

Being fit helps Ada's asthma because it means her lungs work really well.

"We'll start by warming up," Devon tells Ada. All athletes do exercises to get their muscles warm and ready for some hard work.

Ada stretches all her muscles. Athletes can injure themselves easily. Ada has strained a muscle in her leg. She makes sure she stretches carefully.

Next Ada jogs on the spot. "My chest feels tight and I'm a bit wheezy today," Ada thinks to herself.

It is especially important for people with asthma to warm up properly. Ada's lungs need to work very hard when she runs.

Ada uses her reliever to help her breathing. "Do you feel better?" asks Devon. "I'll be fine, thank you," Ada tells him.

Ada uses her reliever before she races. She takes a big breath in, then holds it as long as possible before letting it out slowly.

Today Ada practises getting off to a good start. "A fast start can win the race," Devon tells her. Ada gets into starting position with her feet on the "starting blocks".

"Go!" shouts Devon and Ada sets off and runs as quickly as she can.

"Well done," says Devon. "Now we'll warm down." It is just as important for athletes to relax their muscles. Ada and Devon jog around the track to warm down.

There are many different things that may cause a person to have an asthma attack such as cold weather, animal fur or pollen.

11

Next Ada uses some
weights to build up
her strength.
Her legs need to
be really powerful.

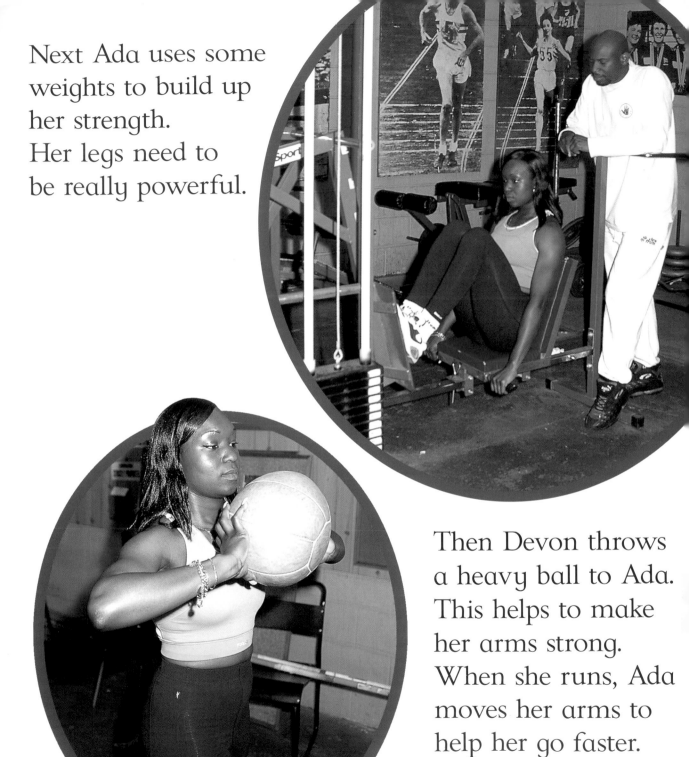

Then Devon throws
a heavy ball to Ada.
This helps to make
her arms strong.
When she runs, Ada
moves her arms to
help her go faster.

After training Ada goes home for lunch.
She has chicken and rice. "This will give you
lots of energy for your race," says Ada's mum.

For a few people, eating certain foods may cause them to have problems with their breathing. If this happens they need to avoid these foods at all times.

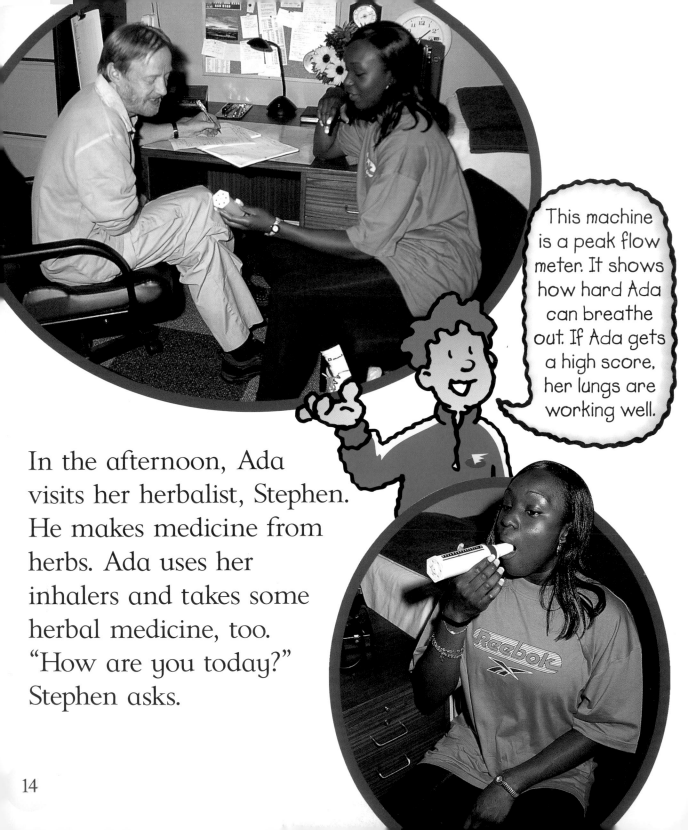

This machine is a peak flow meter. It shows how hard Ada can breathe out. If Ada gets a high score, her lungs are working well.

In the afternoon, Ada visits her herbalist, Stephen. He makes medicine from herbs. Ada uses her inhalers and takes some herbal medicine, too. "How are you today?" Stephen asks.

14

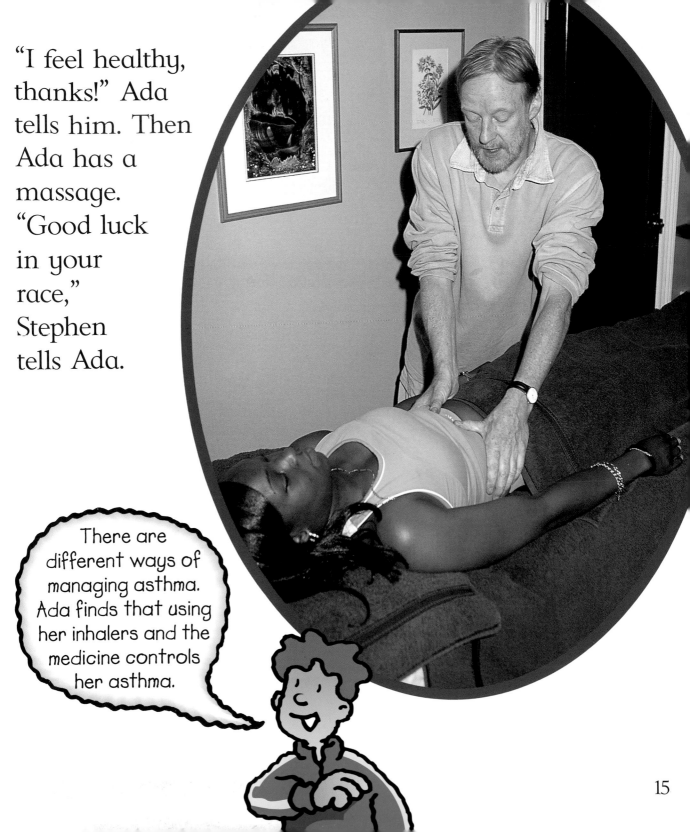

"I feel healthy, thanks!" Ada tells him. Then Ada has a massage. "Good luck in your race," Stephen tells Ada.

There are different ways of managing asthma. Ada finds that using her inhalers and the medicine controls her asthma.

Later on, it's time for the race. At the track, Ada puts on her running shoes. They are a special shape and have spikes on their soles to grip the track.

Ada uses her reliever about 20 minutes before the race to stop her having any asthma symptoms.

The girls position themselves
on the "starting blocks".
"I must remember this morning's
training," Ada thinks to herself.
The starter pistol goes and
they're off!

Ada gets a good start and runs as fast as she can. She concentrates as she runs.

Ada wins the race! "Yes!" laughs Ada as she crosses the finish line.

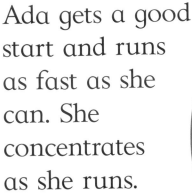

Having asthma means that Ada thinks about her breathing more than other athletes. But it doesn't stop her winning races!

Ada wins a gold medal.
"I'm so excited!" she thinks. "I've won!"

So you want to be an athlete?

1. Join a local club. It takes a lot of practice to become a medal winner.

2. Start getting fit! You will need lots of energy.

3. You will need special running shoes called "spikes" and "starting blocks" to practise with. These can be expensive so try to get a local business to sponsor you.

4. Remember, sometimes you will run as part of a team, not just for yourself. You might even run for your country!

5. There are different athletic sports. If you are not a runner, try the high jump, long jump or throwing the javelin or discus!

Facts about asthma

- Asthma is very common and there seem to be more and more people with it every year.

- Asthma is usually triggered by something. Ada finds her asthma is worse when the weather is cold. Other triggers include colds and infections, pollen from plants and flowers and fur.

- Asthma affects the airways which take air into and out of your lungs. The airways are red and swollen and react badly to certain triggers.

- Some people may need to use inhalers more often than others. Ada always uses hers before a race.

How you can help

If you are with someone when they have an asthma attack, stay calm. Get them to sit up straight and breathe slowly. You can breathe slowly at the same time to help them. A bad asthma attack can be very dangerous.

Ask them where their reliever is. Some people call them 'puffers'. If they find it hard to breathe after a few minutes of using their reliever, call 999 and ask for an ambulance.

Remember to think of people who have asthma in your everyday life. If you have a friend who has asthma try to think ahead and avoid the things that trigger an attack.

Addresses and further information

National Asthma Campaign
and **Junior Asthma Club (for children
aged 4-13 years with asthma and their friends)**
Providence House
Providence Place
London
N1 0NT
Asthma Helpline 0845 7 01 02 03 (Mon-Fri 9 a.m.– 7 p.m.)
Website: http//www.asthma.org.uk

**REACH National Advice Centre for
Children with Reading Difficulties**
Nine Mile Ride
California Country Park
Finchampstead, RG40 4HT

National Asthma Campaign
Level 1,
Palmerston Crescent
South Melbourne
VIC 3205
Australia

Index

© 2000 Franklin Watts

Franklin Watts
96 Leonard Street
London
EC2A 4XD

Franklin Watts Australia
14 Mars Road
Lane Cove
NSW 2066

ISBN: 0 7496 3669 6

Dewey Decimal Classification
Number: 362.4

10 9 8 7 6 5 4 3 2 1

A CIP catalogue record for
this book is available from the
British Library.

Printed in Malaysia

Consultants: National Asthma Campaign;
Beverley Mathias, REACH.
Editor: Samantha Armstrong
Designer: Louise Snowdon
Photographer: Chris Fairclough
Illustrator: Derek Matthews

With thanks to: Ada Nwosu and her family,
her trainer Devon Wright, and the National
Asthma Campaign.